CW00536936

THE LITTLE BOOK OF
AUDI
QUATTRO

Written by Charlie Morgan and Stan Fowler

THE LITTLE BOOK OF
AUDI
QUATTRO

This edition first published in the UK in 2008
By Green Umbrella Publishing

© Green Umbrella Publishing 2008

www.gupublishing.co.uk

Publishers: Jules Gammond and Vanessa Gardner

All rights reserved. No part of this work may be
reproduced or utilised in any form or by any means,
electronic or mechanical, including photocopying,
recording or by any information storage and retrieval
system, without prior written permission of the publisher.

Printed and bound in China

ISBN 978-1-906635-53-4

The views in this book are those of the author but they are general views
only and readers are urged to consult the relevant and qualified specialist
for individual advice in particular situations.

Green Umbrella Publishing hereby exclude all liability to the extent
permitted by law of any errors or omissions in this book and for any loss,
damage or expense (whether direct or indirect) suffered by a third party
relying on any information contained in this book.

All our best endeavours have been made to secure copyright clearance for
every photograph used but in the event of any copyright owner being
overlooked please address correspondence to Green Umbrella Publishing
The Old Bakehouse, 21 The Street, Lydiard Millicent, Swindon SN5 3LU

Contents

4 – 13   The Beginnings Of A Famous History

14 – 27   The History Of Audi

28 – 29   Dr Ferdinand Piech

30 – 35   Jorg Bensinger And Walter Treser

36 – 55   Quattro Coupé

56 – 61   Sports Quattro

62 – 69   Rallying

70 – 99   The Races: A History

100 – 115   The Rally Drivers

116 – 125   The Quattro In A Modern World

Chapter 1

The Beginnings Of A Famous History

RIGHT The corporate logo for Audi AG

LIKE MANY CAR MANUFACTURERS, Audi AG have had a chequered history with customary highs and lows. While some of the company's cars have waned into insignificance, there is one that particularly stands out from the crowd; the Audi Quattro. From its debut in the 1980s, the Quattro was set to steal the show and it did just that on both road and track. Today, it is a much loved classic with fans and Quattro enthusiasts the world over. Originally, Audi had intended to produce just 400 Quattros to be used in Rally driving, (although there were other expectations within the company). In the end, nearly 11,500 vehicles were built for a hungry export market.

The car was unveiled at the Geneva Motor Show in March 1980 and as the first four-wheel drive grand tourer since 1966 it caused a sensation. Taking its name from the Italian word "Quattro", meaning four, the car became one of the most significant Rally cars of all time when it was one of the first to take advantage of the changed rules in competition racing allowing a four-wheel drive to participate. Critics were sceptical that a four-wheel drive could achieve as near as much momentum, power and versatility as other vehicles and labelled them, incorrectly, as too heavy and complex. They were to be proved wrong.

Officially, the car was simply known

as "Quattro" and the word became synonymous with any Audi four-wheel drive system, but the Quattro was also known as the ur-Quattro, the German translation meaning "original". The first taste of the car's special capabilities were unleashed to the public in late 1980 in Europe. The car, both on and off the track, was to prove instrumental in turning around the fortunes of the four-ringed motif company that had almost, but not quite, been forgotten.

Vorsprung durch Technik is almost as common in English (through advertising) today as it is in Germany. Meaning "advancement through technology" the phrase was coined by Audi AG for branding all their manufactured cars. It was certainly true of the Quattro which astounded spectators at the 1983 International RAC Rally held at Weston Park in November that year. The speed and the agility of the vehicle, not to mention the car's cornering capabilities left onlookers speechless one moment and bursting into spontaneous applause the next. Nothing like it had ever been witnessed before. The days of Ford's Escort twin-cam domination looked like they were well and truly over.

The Quattro was developed using

LEFT The Quattro made its debut at the Geneva Motor Show in 1980

four-wheel drive technology that had previously been devised for Volkswagen's military vehicle, the Iltis. Suggested by chassis engineer Jorg Bensinger, the idea quickly took off and the Quattro was the first German large-scale production vehicle to feature permanent four-wheel drive through a centre differential. Achieving 0-100 kph in 7.1 seconds, the sports car wasn't just a sensation at the Geneva Motor Show. Its road holding was second to none and it had 11 exciting years in production. Today, as so many Audis have been called Quattros, enthusiasts use the term ur-Quattro to refer to the original car. The story for Audi began with forward thinking Bensinger who had spent time in Finland with the Iltis where he witnessed its incredible off-road ability and its capabilities in snow conditions. He contacted Audi's director of technical development, Ferdinand Piech, in February 1977 and suggested that the Audi 80 be developed to incorporate four-wheel drive. Piech was particularly excited by the idea, so Bensinger, in collaboration with Walter Treser, director of pre-development and other team members began work on what was to become one of the most innovative

ideas on the motoring scene. Code-named A1, or "Allrad 1", the prototype was designed with a transmission similar to the Iltis, courtesy of Hans Nedvidek. By September that same year, the project was given the blessing of the Audi board and was renamed "Entwicklungsarbeit 262" (EA 262). However, permission to go ahead with the project was still required from Audi's parent company and to convince the "powers that be" that it was essential to continue, never mind worth it, a test was carried out over one of the highest roads in Europe. The place chosen was the Turracher Hohe where some of the pass has more than a 30 per cent gradient.

Following the test, Ernst Fiala, Volkswagen's group development director allowed his wife to use the vehicle for a shopping trip in Vienna, or so the story goes. Mrs Fiala complained that the car "hopped" and was particularly difficult to park and so a centre differential seemed to be an essential missing ingredient. Hans Nedvidek and Franz Tengler were charged with the task of devising the structure and came up with yet another inspirational solution. What they actually did was drive another Audi

80 differential, placed longitudinally, via a hollow propshaft. The idea was simple, but incredibly efficient.

Sharing the same chassis as the Coupe GT, the Quattro had some unique features. These differences didn't just include the permanent four-wheel drive, but also a fuel-injected turbo engine (160 bhp which was quickly increased to 200 bhp), Audi 200 brakes and two extra lockable differentials.

The price was just as impressive at DM 49,500 (approximately £12,000). As other models based on the same chassis were around DM 25,000, it was a significant increase. Despite the expense, more than 11,000 Quattros were sold by the end of the year it made its debut. But, these were more than just production cars; each one was a time-consum-

ABOVE Vorsprung durch Technik has been used in advertising campaigns since the 1970s

ing effort of hand built quality and beauty. Built at the Ingolstadt factory, the car's team consigned to building the Quattros on weekdays only (the rest of Audi production took place over seven days a weeks, 24 hours a day) numbered just 46. Each car took a total of 40 hours labour over seven days to build and approximately three a day left the factory. The tests that the finished cars then endured were no less impressive.

Each was put through rigorous checks to ensure that the engine and suspension was correct. Then, the cars were put through a test drive on a stand before taking to the public roads. Next came the test track and any vehicle involved in an accident while testing was scrapped. The testing was stringent and no other manufacturer at the time apart from Porsche was known to put its cars through such checks. Although somewhat primitive in today's motoring environment, the Quattro was the first high-performance car to have electronic engine management. Other standard features included Goodyear tyres, power steering, front and rear fog lights, tinted windows, hydraulically assisted brakes and headlight washers.

One year after its launch in Geneva, the Quattro made its debut on the UK market and the first shipment contained 163 vehicles. The cars, however, were left-hand drive. It wasn't long before Audi began incorporating electric windows and central locking in their cars. The first six Audi dealers in the UK were all given specialist training in demonstrating their new cars and conversions to right-hand drive – despite Audi's insistence that this wasn't possible – soon began to appear on the market. In a move that was to help Audi achieve one of its most successful export markets, the company began building right-hand drive cars towards the end of 1983, however, the brakes remained firmly on the left-hand side and were worked by a pushrod that ran behind the heater from the driver's pedal. Also in 1983, Patrizia (a voice synthesiser) was added and by the following year, the leather steering wheel and revised dashboard had appeared.

The only external changes to the Quattro came in 1985 when the vertical front grill was replaced with a sloping one. This was accompanied by sloping headlights and smoked rear lights. This was also the year that Audi began using

LEFT The Quattro's technology was based on the Volkswagen Iltis

RIGHT The prototype being tested in arctic conditions

badges of the logo and label rather than transfers. Other minor changes occurred over the preceding years making the car more luxurious and comfortable with added extras and features fitted for optimum performance. Of all the Quattros, a large proportion of enthusiasts were unanimous in rating the MB ur-Quattro as one of the best.

Despite rising demand, Audi had wanted to discontinue the Quattro by the beginning of 1989. The only reason that the car continued to sell was the backlog of outstanding orders that the company was obliged to fulfil. Until the arrival of the Quattro, consumers only had experience of four-wheel drives belonging to fairly mundane, but useful utility vehicles. Here was something new, something exciting that would rewrite the rule book in more ways than one. People still rave, and rightly so, about the Quattro today. It is unsurpassed in its forward thinking vision and despite the fact that Audi stopped making them, it is still highly regarded as one of the best cars of all time and has a place in the hearts of many motorists. It is, undoubtedly, one of the "classics" of the classic cars.

Chapter 2

A History Of Audi

RIGHT August Horch, a board member of the Auto Union AG, at the end of the 1930s

AUDI HAS TAKEN A LONG AND often lonely road to achieving optimum success. The company can trace its beginnings back to 1899 and August Horch who produced his first car two years later in 1901. Born in the German municipality of Winningen on 12 October 1868, Horch was an engineer and a pioneer of the motoring industry in his homeland. After finishing his education in Mittweida, the young Horch began his illustrious career with Karl Benz, the widely regarded inventor of the gasoline-powered car. Benz (1844-1929) was a German engine designer and engineer who patented his work before his contemporaries, Gottlieb Daimler and Wilhelm Maybach, could do the same. It was reported that all three innovators were working on similar projects and Benz was granted a patent for his first engine

in 1878. Horch joined Benz in 1896 but in November 1899 he left his mentor to establish A Horch & Cie in Cologne, Germany. Having set up operations in Reichenbach, Horch then moved the company to Zwickau. However, a dispute in 1909 forced the founding member of the company out and Horch set up a rival company called Horch Automobilwerke GmbH.

Unfortunately, or perhaps fortunately for Audi enthusiasts the world over, legal proceedings decreed that Horch was no longer able to maintain his own name for his company and he changed the manufacturing name in 1910 to Audi Automobilwerke GmbH; Audi being the Latin name for Horch, which in German means "hark" or "listen". This name was the brainchild of Franz Fikentscher's son, who had been studying Latin in the room, when the two

RIGHT Auto Union
Type C, 1936

men met with others to discuss the naming crisis.

The cars that Horch's new company manufactured were a success, especially in sporting events (perhaps a sign of things to come). In August 1928 a majority stake in Audiwerke was acquired by the Danish engineer, Jorgen Skafte Rasmussen, originally from DKW and just four years later, in June 1932, a merger took place that would bring the four-ringed symbol to the world's attention. Rasmussen with DKW, Horch and Wanderer (the German manufacturer of cars, vans, motorcycles and other machinery) all joined forces to create Auto Union, which was perhaps most renowned for its racing team "Auto Union Rennabteilung" based in Zwickau. The company's racing team was the main contender for all the established championships alongside Mercedes-Benz who were their main rival throughout the 1930s racing scene. Such was the interest from the press of these two opposing teams that each was named the Silver Arrows. In fact, the power of these vehicles and their superior expertise meant that the records they set from 1934 onwards (particularly in 1937 with

unlimited models) were only equalled in the early 1980s when turbo-charged Grand Prix cars of Formula 1 came into existence.

At this time, the four-ringed symbol, representing the four amalgamated companies, was only used for Auto Union racing and each member company retained their own emblems and names for car manufacturing and sales. Technical development was swift and became extremely complicated and

LEFT The Auto Union
Streamliner

concentrated. Some Audi models
housed Horch or Wanderer built
engines but the outbreak of the Second
World War would see a different type of
vehicle introduced; the armoured car.
The Sd-Kfz 222's were light armoured
vehicles – four-wheel drive – which
were to become the mainstay of Hitler's
Nazi Germany replacing the Sd-Kfz 250
which had excelled as a reconnaissance
vehicle in Western Europe but had suffered from poor off-road performance

RIGHT The Sd-Kfz 222

on the Eastern Front and North Africa. The Sd-Kfz 222 had a top speed of 50 mph with its Horch/Auto Union V8 engine. This wasn't Horch's only contribution to the war effort. He also built the Kraftfahrzeug or Kfz 11 (also known as the Horch Type 80) which was used to ferry German military officials safely around occupied territories.

It wasn't all success for Horch and Auto Union during the Second World War. Large parts of the Auto Union plants were bombed heavily (and partly destroyed) during hostilities and after war ended, Zwickau – the company's home – was no longer part of Saxony. It became a slice of the German Democratic Republic and Auto Union was broken down into smaller companies and renamed "VEB Automobilwerk Zwickau". This new company, however, retained its own name when it launched in Ingolstadt. Previous employees moved from Zwickau to Ingolstadt and production was soon underway once again, this time, under the DKW label. Cars in production at this time were based on a pre-war, two-stroke engine design.

Things were set to change for Auto Union in 1958 when 87 per cent of the company was acquired by Daimler-Benz. The new investor then bought the company out fully the following year. But in 1964, another car manufacturer came on the scene in the guise of Volkswagen who bought the Ingolstadt factory and all the brands of Auto

Union. It was at this time that the faithful two-stroke engines finally met their match. Many customers preferred the more luxurious four-stroke engines and Volkswagen passed over the DKW branding and launched "Audi". The first model off the production line was the F103, known simply as the Audi originally before it was marketed as the Audi 72. It was followed by the Audi 60, 75, 80 and Super 90; all so-called in reference to their horsepower. These became popular models until the early 1970s. Having previously merged with NSU,

the former giant in motorcycle manufacturing, at the end of the 1960s, Auto Union pulled the company from Neckarsulm out of a rut. NSU had, in fact, been a company ahead of its time with its NSU Ro 80; a car designed using aerodynamics and lightweight bodywork. However, problems with the rotary engine that had been a specific focus of the company led to its merger with the more successful Auto Union. The NSU K70 – designed somewhere in between the company's previous cars and the Ro 80 – signalled the end of the NSU brand when Volkswagen claimed the car for their own.

Once again, another new name was in the offing. This time the company became Audi NSU Auto Union AG and Audi began to become a brand in its own right since before the war. It was then introduced, as a brand, into the US market in 1970. The 1968 Audi 100 was the first car manufactured, quickly followed by the Audi 80, or Fox, four years later and the Audi 50; which later metamorphosed into the Volkswagen Polo. The company had a solid, if somewhat conservative image during the early 1970s, despite the fact that the Audi 50 was fast developing into the Polo and

LEFT Pictured clockwise NSU Ro 80, NSU Prinz 100 TT, NSU Prinz 4, Audi 75 Variant, NSU 1200, Audi 60 L, Audi 100 LS, Audi 100 Coupé S (centre)

paving the way for one of Volkswagen's most world-renowned cars, the Golf.

Audi chassis engineer Jorg Bensinger put forward the proposal that the company try developing a four-wheel drive for the range to enhance Rally performance. As already discussed, originally this concept had been used in the Iltis military vehicle and the engineer's proposal was readily agreed to. It was to be the start of something big for the company who didn't have a particularly high profile at the time. The high performance car was the "Quattro" which was ready for the world motor shows in 1980.

Just five years after the Quattro made its first appearance, NSU and Auto Union brands were no more and the company changed its name to Audi AG. The following year, in 1986, the Audi 80 was gaining a reputation as an old man's car and so, the Audi 89 was launched which proved extremely popular, although somewhat basic. As a result, the Audi 90 made its debut and set out from the start to provide a more superior type of vehicle. Meanwhile, sales of the Audi 80 were beginning to slump and company efforts were further hampered by a biased programme in the US called *60 Minutes* which reported that all brands of Audi

suffered from acceleration problems. Unfortunately for Audi, the programme did not concentrate on the true facts and geneRally sensationalised the issues for optimum viewing. Luckily for the company, the same problems were not encountered in the European market which points to the fact that drivers here had more widespread experience of manual transmissions, whereas US drivers were used to brake and accelerator pedals with a far greater distance between the two. Audi seriously considered pulling out of the US market until a smart, stylish new model – the Audi A4 – began a turnaround in sales revenue across the Atlantic when the car was released in 1996.

Today, Audi enjoys successful sales the world over with its current models which include the extremely popular A3, the A4, A5, A6, A8, Q7, Allroad Quattro, RS4, R8, S3, S4, S5, S6, the S8 and the TT. From humble beginnings in a small town in Germany the company started by August Horch, has grown to become one of the most successful, dynamic and instantly recognisable car manufacturers with its unmistakable four-ringed symbol. The last Audi Quattro left the factory in May 1991.

LEFT Audi Quatro on display

Chapter 3

Dr Ferdinand Piech

RIGHT Dr Ferdinand
Piech, father of the
Quattro idea

THE GRANDSON OF FERDINAND Porsche, Dr Ferdinand Piech was born in Vienna, Austria on 17 April 1937. With a degree in mechanical engineering and a thesis about the development of a Formula 1 engine, Piech was destined for great things. When he graduated from ETH Zurich in Switzerland in 1962 he worked for Porsche in Stuttgart, Germany, on developing the Porsche 906 and the later models that eventually culminated in the highly successful Porsche 917. In 1972, he joined Audi at the plant in Ingolstadt where he quickly worked his way up to manager of technological engineering in 1975. Under Piech, the Audi 80 and Audi 100 were born and in 1977 with a proposal from his chassis engineer, the concept of the Audi Quattro began to take shape. Using a five-cylinder engine, for which there was a demand, was almost child's play for Piech who had

been busy developing a five-cylinder engine at his own engineering company before he joined Audi.

Piech eventually became chairman and chief executive officer of Volkswagen AG in 1993. It was a role he continued until his retirement in 2002. However, he remains on the Supervisory Board as chairman where he serves as an advisor. In his last two years with the Volkswagen Group, Piech also chaired the board of Scania AB. It was Piech who was responsible for driving the company upmarket – both with Volkswagen and Audi brands – and he was responsible for Audi's purchase of Lamborghini which established Bugatti Automobiles SAS. This positive move was balanced by the controversial intended purchase of Rolls-Royce and Bentley. Volkswagen were denied the Rolls-Royce name

which eventually went to BMW. One of Piech's outstanding achievements during his long and distinguished career with the group was his resilience to rescue Volkswagen's failing North American market. This was achieved with the manufacture of the new Beetle which was introduced in 1998. Piech was an aggressive, but outstanding manager who had big ideas and the ability to make his ambitions a reality. Today, the father of 13 children owns a significant share of his grandfather's company, Porsche.

Chapter 4

Jorg Bensinger And Walter Treser

RIGHT Jorg Bensinger, project leader of the Audi Quattro

BORN IN 1937, JORG BENSINGER joined Audi in 1968 having clocked up extensive experience with other motoring giants, Mercedes-Benz, BMW and Porsche. He was passionate about the four-wheel drive vehicles and was particularly desperate that an opportunity at Audi should present itself to include the revolutionary idea. He was joined by Walter Treser, the director of pre-development, Dr Fritz Naumann, head of general vehicle development and Hans Nedvidek, who was retired but remained as a consultant for Audi alongside Franz Tengler. Undoubtedly, the project was Bensinger's passion, and as an experienced engineer, no one would dispute that he was running the

Quattro show. It was the Audi intention that it would build Quattro versions of every model in the then current range and this helped to raise Bensinger's profile considerably in the company. In 1984 he was appointed as senior manager, chassis and suspension research and development. He was certain of the benefits of four-wheel drive in high performance cars and strongly believed that only permanent 4x4 had anything to offer. He was no fan of part-time four-wheel drive. What Bensinger and his team managed to do was completely revolutionise the concept of four-wheel drive.

It was customary for Audi to use a longitudinal engine and gearbox layout.

Using the 4x4 concept, in fact, worked rather well with the design. Luckily for Bensinger, the UK was a staunch supporter of high performance cars being given four-wheel drive and it wouldn't be long before the 4x4 was not just the all-terrain vehicle of the farming and forestry communities. Unlike the Jensen FF that failed in the late 1960s due to its high fuel consumption required for its large V8 engine, the Quattro was destined for success. There were some marketing issues to be overcome first, however. Audi had long been lagging behind the likes of rivals BMW who had cleverly jumped on the back of the Thatcher government's concept of hard work and prosperity. The middle classes of the UK in the late 1970s and 1980s all wanted to own BMWs. They had become the status symbol of the masses; to own one meant you had arrived. Piech was somewhat worried that Audi may not be taken seriously if it tried to revolutionise a car, that priced accordingly and had already been built, was aimed at exactly that market. Although Bensinger wasn't overly worried about the full marketability of the car, Ferdinand Piech was adamant that the car should be able to perform on and off

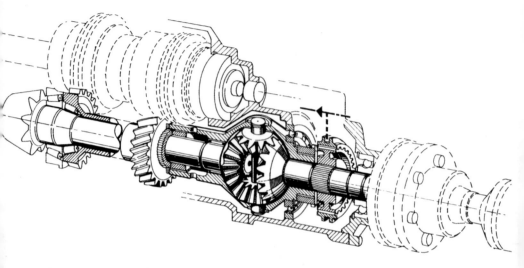

ABOVE The Quattro
drive principle

RIGHT Quattro V1

road. Arguably, his foresight turned out to be the correct course for the car to follow. The Audi 80 was the chosen subject and the Iltis 4x4 transmission was applied. Proceedings took place under the supervision of the Quattro driving force, Walter Treser. The outstanding driver, born on 18 April 1940, had cars in his blood and was instrumental in seeing the Quattro to fruition. He is also credited with giving the revolutionary vehicle its name.

When the Audi Quattro team needed to impress the Volkswagen parent com-

pany, they invited board members to join them on the track at Turracher Hohe in January 1978. The idea was to convince the board that the conventional tyres on a four-wheel drive vehicle had incredible benefits in icy, snowy weather with steep gradients.

The treacherous weather conditions on the day helped to ensure that the Quattro would go into production as astounded board members watched the car's performance.

Treser's credentials with BMW and DKW had earned him an undisputable reputation and he became as keen as Bensinger to see the Quattro make it onto the racetrack and into the market-place. He joined Audi in the same year that Quattro was more than just a concept (1977) having moved from Daimler-Benz where he had spent 14 years as a test driver. He began for Audi as a pre-development director and then became competitions manager when the Quattro went into racing. It was an extremely testing time for Treser who

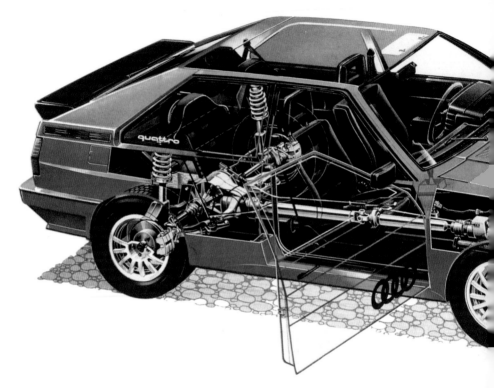

would be hailed a hero along with the rest of the team should the car make the grade, however, he was also well aware that the failure would be his should the project flounder. Although the Quattro was a resounding success, there were pitfalls and Treser was sacked by Piech some 18 months after the Quattro first

appeared on a racetrack. In 1982, Treser began his own business in Quattros but his passion was to build a sports car. He needed a great deal of money and, sadly, the project failed and operations were ground to a halt in a 1988 court order. However, in 1992, Treser became competitions manager at GM-Opel.

As a racing car, the Quattro's future was assured, but the conversion to a mainstream market required a few adjustments. Ferdinand Piech had made a provision that the four-wheel drive Quattro needed to succeed on dry tarmac as well as in an icy, snow-covered environment. It was an objective that

needed to be met if the Quattro was ever to be driven from a car showroom. The engineers working on the A1 prototype achieved their goal in 1978 when the car was test driven at the Hockenheim track against a Porsche 928 V8 sports coupe. The Porsche was undoubtedly the more powerful car, but tests showed that there was little in the difference of timing between the two cars. Rather reluctantly Dr Ernst Fiala approved that the car could go into production, however, the centre differential had become a pre-requisite. Another bonus for the Quattro prototype was the support of the Finnish Rally driver Hannu Mikkola who, after testing the car, immediately signed up to drive the Quattro in the Rally world championship events in 1981. It was a huge boost for the team and Audi in general. With time of the essence and demands from Piech about certain features, design and objectives, there was also the added pressure of ensuring that the car would be ready for the 1980 world motor shows. There were 12 prototypes built over the two years prior to launch and although many cars featured at motor shows are never built, the Quattro would prove an exception.

Chapter 5

Quattro Coupé

THE ARRIVAL OF THE AUDI QUATtro at the 1980 Geneva Motor Show was hailed as the most sensational launch of a new car since Jaguar's E-type had been unveiled 19 years previously. Many who visited the Audi stand simply didn't believe that the German company would have the nerve to mass produce a car which, in their opinion, would not sell in sufficient numbers. How wrong they were…

The Quattro has been described as having been put together from Audi's parts bin but, while there is some truth in the way that the various components were borrowed from other cars, it was the sum of the parts not the individual ingredients that went into making such a classic car.

The bodyshell was created with a floor-pan lifted from the Audi 80 that was combined with a modified coupé superstructure that contained seating for five. Although there was plenty of headroom, the width left something to be desired (especially if you intended to seat three adults in the back). The engine – more of which later – was the 2,144cc five-cylinder 10-valve lump that powered the Audi 200 Turbo, although it was redeveloped from 170 PS to 200 PS and claimed a higher turbocharger boost. This unit (German for Pferdestärke or "horse strength") is no longer a statutory unit, but is still commonly used in Europe, South America and Japan. Rendered obsolete by EEC directives, when it was replaced by the kilowatt as the official power measuring unit, one PS is the equivalent of 0.98632 hp.

The transmission was a real mishmash of Audi in that the gearbox and clutch came from the Audi 100/200, the 4x4 design was pinched from the Iltis

ABOVE The Audi
Coupé Quattro 1984

while an Audi 50/80 central diff was integrated into the gearbox. The Iltis donated its real axle components and lock differential while the 100/200 was the basis for the front diff. Audi did have to create a new two-piece propshaft but the driveshafts were modified existing units. The majority of the remaining parts such as gearbox housing, the gear-change mechanism and synchromesh were again utilised from the 100/200. The MacPherson strut suspension was drawn from the 80/100/200 cars with the front coil springs being donated by the 80 and the rear springs courtesy of the 200 Turbo. The Quattro benefited from power assisted steering and Girling disc brakes all round with ABS after September 1983.

The engine itself had been developed to a high standard and as such was unique when fitted to a petrol-powered car. Modifications had brought the power output from the five-cylinder turbocharged lump up from 170 PS to 200 PS while it also boasted the latest in intercooling and electronic engine management.

The engine that had been installed in the 200 had been a non-intercooled ver-

sion that Audi had proudly stated would offer 170 PS when it was launched in September 1979. But the engineers realised that there was untapped potential in this unit and set about modifying it to Rally specifications. The strength of the single overhead camshaft engine was in its six-main bearing bottom end but they managed to raise the output from the 200's 79.3 PS/litre to the 93.3 PS/litre that would power the Quattro. This resulted in optimum power being achieved at 5,500 rpm instead of 5,300 rpm.

The addition of an intercooler and boosting of the turbocharger, aided by a revised inlet manifold and enlarged exhaust were also responsible for greatly improving the performance. Although the exhaust pipes were constructed from stainless steel, the silencer boxes weren't and these proved costly to replace once rusted through.

Like so many other cars, the Quattro suffered as a result of US legislation so Transatlantic customers had to be happy with 40 HP less as a result of equipment that was added to adhere to strict emissions guidelines. This had a drastic effect on sales in America as the public didn't want a watered

LEFT Audi Quattro, 2.2 litre five-cylinder turbo engine, 148 kW, 200 bhp, 1982

RIGHT The Audi Quattro which won the 52nd MonteCarlo Rally in 1984

down version of the car that all Europe was raving about.

The external styling of the Quattro was the responsibility of Martin Smith. Born in Sheffield in 1949, Smith had been fanatical about cars since he was a young boy and had even written to Alec Issigonis – designer of the iconic Mini – asking for advice on how to become a car designer. As a result of the reply he received, Smith studied Engineering at the University of Liverpool before graduating with a Masters degree in Vehicle Design from the Royal College of Art in London.

Smith's automotive career began with Porsche in 1973 before moving to Audi in 1977. A short-lived stint with BMW followed before he returned to the Audi family where he spent the remainder of the 1980s and the majority of the 1990s. His last task before leaving Audi for a second time was to come up with the interior design for the first generation Audi TT, after which he moved to General Motors and Ford.

Smith also worked on Audi's concept Avus Quattro that was previewed at the 1991 Tokyo Motor Show. The Avus was envisaged with a geometric style and utilised aluminium in its construction.

The engine that was to be installed, however, was still under development so a carefully painted reconstruction of wood and plastic was housed in the engine bay.

Working within strict constraints, Smith – under the supervision of Hartmut Warkuss – was given a brief by Dr Piech to create a very technical, very functional but commercially viable body for the Quattro but within an extremely tight budget. This meant that they did not have the option of changing the basic body shape of the original coupé. As it was, they modified various body panels to accommodate the wider track and four-wheel drive equipment.

The cost implications dictated that any such modifications could not be rendered in sheet metal so polyurethane and plastics were added to the standard panels. The flared wheel arches made the Quattro 41 mm wider than the standard coupé while the chunkier colour-coded bumpers increased the length by 55 mm. With the addition of a rear spoiler to the boot lid, these modifications became increasingly popular as bodykits became a huge aftersales phenomenon for many models as other manufacturers joined the bandwagon.

LEFT The Audi Quattro A2 and S1 Quattro, 1984

The rack and pinion steering system that Audi designed for the Quattro was so perfect that many claim the company were unable to recreate its performance for the next quarter of a century. The steering featured an ATE pump to provide high pressure hydraulic assistance and there was also a central reservoir to help the brake servos.

Wheels came courtesy of a 15" alloy with 16 spokes or a forged five spoke version that helped the Quattro perform superbly in early Rallying events. If you happened to suffer a puncture, then there was a spacesaver wheel that would enable you to limp to a garage for repairs although this was later replaced with a full-size spare as many owners complained.

Despite the fact that Audi only originally intended to manufacture around 400 Quattros, order levels by November 1980 had shown how inaccurate their estimate had been. The regulations for the car to be entered into the Group 4 World Rally Championship was satisfied by the end of the year enabling it to compete in the 1981 season and within two years of its launch, the Quattro passed the 2,000 figure mark. This was, of course, partly instigated by the intense media speculation in the run up to the launch.

One of the main problems that Audi had to overcome was where the new model would be manufactured and the fact that, initially at least, the cars were assembled by hand clearly indicated that the numbers of cars being finished on a daily basis would be low. The solution was to create a partitioned assembly line in a side hall at Ingolstadt, coincidentally alongside the one that built the Iltis from which the 4x4 idea had originated.

The bodies were welded together in another part of the factory but, while individual panels were galvanised, the complete shell never received this treatment and was therefore prone to deterioration at the hands of the elements. It is perhaps slightly baffling that this was never considered because in all other areas of manufacturing the Quattro, Audi were somewhat perfectionists.

The assembly line consisted of 22 people who took such pride in their work that half of them remained with the original Quattro for the 11 years of its production. In other areas, the engines were put together and then tested for torque, power and emissions

while the completed cars each went through a rigorous road test. These stringent quality checks ensured that the Quattro was more reliable and better finished than many of its rivals.

As the first cars were designated for the German market, they were all natuRally left-hand drive. Indeed, it would take a few years for a right-hand drive option to become available although some special-ist companies did offer to carry out a conversion for British owners.

Audi paid great attention to the detail of the Quattro. Paint finishes on offer included metallic Saturn, Helios Blue and Silver Diamond with non-metallic options of Venus Red and plain White. All cars were finished with matt black window frames and door handles along with colour coded bumpers and a red

fluorescent strip across the rear. Indeed, such was the popularity of this strip that accessories companies began manufacturing their own version across which was emblazoned the name of the model it was to be fitted upon.

In line with its Rallying heritage, the two pairs of halogen headlamps came fitted with electric washers and there were two front fog lamps to illuminate the road in adverse weather conditions. While this all sounded fine in theory, the reality was a somewhat dimmer picture that was only rectified in 1983 when one-piece Cibié lights were adopted.

Inside the cockpit, sporty supportive front seats were the order of the day, with the driver's enabling height adjustment as well. They were finished in velour that unfortunately did not wear very well and, while the cars were promoted in such manner as to persuade potential customers that they would easily last for 200,000 miles, sadly the seat trim showed signs of wear and tear a lot earlier. Bronzed (or optional green) glass all round added to the air of excellence, while the laminated windscreen was ahead of its time in that it included a darkened strip running

LEFT 1985 Audi S1 Quattro

RIGHT The lightweight
aluminium bodyshell
prototype, 1985

across the top.

The dashboard's standard instrumentation saw a fuel and turbo boost gauge nestled between the rev counter and speedometer while equipment offered on the German models included cruise control, a central locking system and a lift-out sunroof. The UK specification models included electric windows, power assisted steering, electrically heated front seats, a rear wash/wipe and central locking.

When it arrived in Britain, not all of the 350 Audi dealers were authorised to sell the cars although they were permitted to carry out routine service operations. Instead, if you wanted to purchase the car of the moment, you had to go to one of six select Quattro service centres. Sales were relatively slow to start with as the first batch of 163 cars took two years to sell, but the situation was worse in the United States where Audi had hoped that this would be the model that would break the dominance of German rivals BMW and Mercedes-Benz. Sales were disappointing and less than 600 cars were sold during the first two years following its introduction in January 1982.

Now that Audi had the car firmly on the market, it was time to take care of the niggling complaints. One of the main improvements that was introduced was ABS braking. It had been hoped that this system would have been ready to install in the car on its initial release but budgetary and staffing restraints meant that more time was needed to develop it to a sufficient standard. Mind you, the lack of anti-lock brakes certainly made it more interesting for spectators who could watch a skilful driver outmanoeuvre his two-wheel drive opponents but the slightest mistiming often ended up with the car careering off the track. It would take until 1983 for ABS to be fitted to Quattros in Germany with the UK following a year later.

Along with the new Cibié headlights for the 1983 cars came a digital dashboard display. This was not greeted with universal delight but offered the driver the option to switch instantly between imperial (mph) and metric (kph) readouts. It also housed an onboard computer that ran on a 128kb memory chip and could warn the driver about such things as testing the brakes, refilling the washer bottle and low fuel.

The year of 1983 was also when Audi realised that their 4x4 technology

should not be confined to the coupé. They launched a Quattro version of the Audi 80 which was aimed directly at the people who might be considering buying a BMW. Launched at St Moritz, Audi were keen to demonstrate their car's all-round capability at the popular ski resort. Retailing at approximately half the price of the turbocharged coupé, the non-turbo 80 Quattro was obviously not as powerful as its cousin and was offered in two-door (although not in the UK) or four-door format. Many felt that the styling was bland but

it typified saloon car manufacturing in the early to mid-1980s. In some respects, it could quite easily be related to Ford's Mark IV Cortina or Nissan's Bluebird. It seemed that individuality was on the decline as everyone stuck to the same formula.

The chassis and floorpans were basically the same as the standard 80, but modifications had to be made to the central tunnel and rear suspension in order to accommodate the four-wheel drive components. The interior of the car came in for criticism due to its ten-

similar to the real thing, there were those who could not afford the turbocharged car who went to great lengths to add accessories so that their friends and neighbours would think they had the car of their dreams. It was, after all, the era of the "hot hatch" as Ford and Volkswagen had proved with their XR3i and Golf GTi respectively.

The 1985 model saw minor modifications such as an angled radiator grille, revised headlamps and a colour-coded rear spoiler while the rear screen heating elements had been redesigned to spell out the legend "Quattro". Other changes included manufacturing more of the exhaust system in stainless steel in order to give it a longer life – a previous bug bear for customers!

Two years later and the 10-valve engine was revamped from 2,144cc to 2,226cc. Although the power remained the same at 200 PS at 5,500 rpm, the big selling point was that maximum torque was achieved at a lowly 2,250 rpm. This gave the car a huge advantage over its competitors who took longer to build up maximum torque that was handled via a patented Torsen central differential to replace the original that had been borrowed from the Audi 50/80.

dency to wear out quickly and, again, a lack of excitement.

Audi also produced an atmospherically-aspirated version of the coupé which came without the inflated price, the high performance and expensive running costs. While it may have looked

QUATTRO COUPÉ

RIGHT Quattro Sport
Coupé, 1984

(Understanding the relationship between torque, power and engine speed is vital in automotive engineering, concerned as it is with transmitting power from the engine through the drive train to the wheels.) Other refinements to the ECU and fuel system gave better consumption and a smoother ride while the annoying turbo lag had also been addressed.

The Quattro benefited from the advances that had been made with the Sport Quattro and 1989 saw the introduction of the 20-valve 2.2 litre RR twin overhead cam engine. This engine proved to be so far ahead of its time that even after production of the Quattro ceased in 1991 it was still being fitted to other Audis such as the 100, S4, S6 and RS2.

The arrival of the new engine coincided with an interior revamp that saw more comfortable seats (emblazoned with the Quattro logo) installed and a smart, comfortable three spoke steering wheel with a leather rim. Audi had also removed the Quattro tag from the rear of the car as they felt, by now, people shouldn't need reminding about the pedigree. The final Audi Quattros to be offered to the public retailed at a whop-

ping £32,995 and production ceased in the second quarter of 1991 with a total of 11,452 vehicles having been built.

Such had been the impact of the Quattro over the 1980s, that Audi's next offering – the S2 coupé, launched in 1991 – could not match up to its predecessor. Despite inheriting the permanent

Quattro four-wheel drive, the S2 only remained in production for two years. Today, Quattro enthusiasts are divided over which car is best; many still prefer the original 10-valve car that was launched in 1980 while there are those who insist that the Sport Quattro or the later 20-valve coupé is the standout model. Whatever your persuasion, there can be no arguing with the fact that the Audi Quattro – in whatever guise – changed the world of motoring forever and paved the way for a 4x4 revolution. Just look around any car park today and you will see that practically every car manufacturer now offers at least one

RIGHT Audi Quattro S2
Coupé, 1991

Chapter 6

Sports Quattro

RIGHT Audi 90 Quattro

WITH AUDI'S ASPIRATIONS IN THE Group B "supercar" Rallying category came the Sport Quattro. As the regulations stipulated that the majority of the car had to be the same as the road version, the Sport Quattro was designed for Rallying first and foremost so those who took one onto the streets were rewarded with blistering performance. They had to make a minimum of 200 of these vehicles in order to qualify to race and eventually manufactured 214 although it was later revealed that only 164 of these were actually sold to customers before production ceased in March 1986.

The Sport Quattro made its first appearance at the Frankfurt Motor Show in September 1983 and was internationally approved in May the following year. Audi flew journalists out to a Bavarian NATO air force base for the April 1984 launch of the car where Rally drivers Walter Rohrl and Harald Demuth demonstrated the performance capabilities.

With a shorter wheelbase and much more power (road versions were rated at 306 PS while their Rallying counterparts could double that), rumours had been rife of the car's existence since late 1981 when media photographers had glimpsed an early prototype at Ingolstadt. Audi shortened the wheelbase by 320 mm but you had to be very lucky to get your hands on one in the UK. With a price tag of over £50,000, only six were imported and one of those went directly into the Patrick Collection in Birmingham, put together by a fan who snapped up Group B Rally cars when manufacturers were desperate to get rid of them in the mid-1980s.

Nowadays, you will have to fork out a six-figure sum to get hold of a genuine factory Sport Quattro but beware, there

ABOVE The Audi Sport Quattro, 1984

are impostors lurking about as there were a number of original coupes specially converted to the swb format for racing purposes.

While Audi had claimed that the finished car would weigh just 1,000 kg (as opposed to 1,300 kg for the Quattro coupe), the Sport Quattro eventually weighed in at 1,273 kg despite all the glassfibre panels and other weight saving measures that had been taken that included the use of Kevlar (a substance that has been used for a range of purposes from space rocket shields to bullet-proof vests).

So while Audi had reduced the wheelbase by 320 mm, the overall length of the car was only 240 mm shorter due to

That was due largely to the engine that featured an aluminium cylinder block and head rather than traditional iron. The five cylinder 2,133cc lump also boasted a unique twin overhead cam with four valves per cylinder, a revised five-into-one exhaust manifold and a larger turbocharger. To ensure that each and every engine passed the quality assurance checks, they were bench tested for 24 hours at 6,300 rpm as well as another day and night at 7,100 rpm.

But it wasn't just the engine that made the Sport Quattro such an exceptional car. The chassis, suspension and brakes were redeveloped to help the muscle car cope with demanding corners in record time. The body was finished off with flared wheel arches, vents, intakes and louvres that did more than add to the car's overall look...they were functional as well as eye-catching.

Unfortunately for Audi, the Sport Quattro failed to make the big impact on the Rallying scene that had been intended. True, they scored some successes but even with the modified S1 and E2 vehicles they found that some of their competitors had made technological advances that put them in front.

the fact that the engine bay had to be extended in order to fit the intercooler. The width of the car was increased by 80 mm to give a different perspective on the original Quattro that many find was not aesthetically pleasing. Okay, it may not have the classic lines that its cousin boasted, but it certainly wasn't lacking in the performance stakes.

ABOVE The Audi Sport Quattro S1, 1985

Chapter 7

Rallying

RIGHT Michele Mouton and Fabrizia Pons in action in their Audi during the RAC Rally, 1984

THE AUDI QUATTRO AS A RALLY car really did impress and delight, despite some of the earlier teething problems in the mechanics. With its steel two-door coupe and lightweight panelling and five cylinder engine, the Quattro would take the Rallying world by storm and would give the Fords, Porches, Opels and Lancias a run for their money. Ferdinand Piech had been interested in developing Audi's racing philosophy along the same lines as Porsche had developed theirs. He ultimately wanted an Audi that could wow on the racing circuit and then just as easily become an everyday car on the highways and byways. For the Audi engineers this would be a tall order, however, as already discussed earlier, there was one man who thought it was possible.

Porsche had a solid reputation on the racing scene, as did Ferrari and rivals Ford, whose main objective was to bring Ferrari down a peg or two. Throughout the 1960s maintaining cars for optimum racing was an expensive business, although Porsche and Ferrari discovered to their delight with their successes that every penny was worth it. Winning

the most esteemed of races brought free publicity which, in turn, sold vehicles and that, after all, was what most of the publicity was about. Le Mans had belonged to Ferrari for the early part of the 1960s and by the end of the decade Porsche were spending similar amounts as their rivals in order to gain the cov-

eted European titles. Porsche had built the 917 to bring them success, which it did, at Le Mans in 1970 and 1971. It also won all the other competitions until it was effectively banned from the racing scene in 1972. This was a disappointment to Porsche, however, they had achieved their objective and their

salesrooms were literally full of customers clamouring to buy the Porsche 911. The coveted French victories also did much for the company's VW Beetle whose sales rocketed to 1.2 million in one year alone in the early 1970s. As a pivotal figure in the success of the sports 917 and the subsequent sales across the Porsche range, Piech was left with an experience he would not forget and a philosophy that was set to continue when he joined Audi.

Although in the early days the Quattro programme was kept a closely-guarded secret, the idea of Audi racing was not and, like the Porsche 917, i would need an extremely high profile i it was to take off in quite the way Piech expected it to. Power and innovation would not be enough. Style, performance and a huge amount of publicity were just as key to the agenda. The money required to ensure the Quattro could compete in rallying on an international level would be phenomenal, however, should Bensinger and Treser model the winning formula then Audi would surely hit the jackpot.

Overall on the Rallying scene, despite the successes of Ferrari and Porsche, it was Ford who had claimed overall success. Alongside other racing teams presented by the likes of Mercedes-Benz, Fiat, Opel, Peugeot and Citroen, Ford had a solid team for international racing and the Escort had proved the most reliable of the range for Rally racing. It was a light and driver-friendly vehicle that adapted well to the rigours of racing and was popular amongst the drivers with its powerful engine and rear-wheel drive.

Realising the importance of the publicity needed to create a hugely popular model, the team were charged with garnering as much attention for the car at all times. The biggest coup came when Hannu Mikkola agreed to drive the as yet unseen car, for the 1981 season. The

second helping hand that Audi managed was to also secure the services of Frenchwoman Michele Mouton. Both drivers were ready and willing to talk to the press; a huge bonus for the team. Against its rivals, however, the Quattro would be heavier and it was the permanent four-wheel drive which Audi were pitting that would lead them to ultimate success both on and off the track.

Although the early days of Quattro racing were not completely successful, one thing was for sure, four-wheel driving and turbocharged engines were the way forward on the racing scene. It was a revolutionary idea which would change the face of racing for good. With a top speed of 160 mph, the ability to slide around corners even though it was four-wheel drive and its ability to accelerate extremely quickly between 35 mph and 100 mph were the winning ingredients for Audi. The Audi was featured in the Algarve Rally in 1980 driven by Hannu Mikkola. In actual fact, the Quattro was destined as the course car, (i.e. it opened each stage of the Rally) but its high speed and agile performance was second to none and it looked more like an elusive leader than a course car. The Quattro's first actual race came

LEFT Quattro in action, 1985

a year later at the 1981 Austrian Rally and it romped home more than 15 minutes ahead of the rest of the field. Some were still sceptical about the car's ability and were already decided that the win had been more of a fluke than anything else. They were to be proved wrong, although some technical difficulties at the Monte Carlo Rally left sceptics with little doubt that they were right. Next, the Quattro was set for the Swedish Rally and it was down to Mikkola to bring the car home. This he did convincingly despite the best efforts of the Escort driven by the legendary fellow Finn, Ari Vatanen.

Walter Treser found himself at the heart of controversy when the Quattro arrived to compete in Greece at the Acropolis Rally. All three Audi Quattros were disqualified when the team made some modifications amidst a storm of protests to counteract the soaring temperatures. It was not the first event to have witnessed such a high level of protests about cars before a race; it sadly wouldn't be the last. It was the following race that Michele Mouton would win with a clear lead when the Quattro was set to race in San Remo and the team won again at the RAC Rally – a gruelling

four-day event. By now, the sceptic were having to eat their words as th Quattro was convincing the world tha it had what it took to be a Worl Championship racing car. The 198 line-up for Audi still included Mikkol and Mouton but they were joined b Stig Blomqvist whose talents for forme team Saab were indisputable. The thre exceptional drivers won the majority o the season's races for Audi and i brought the company's first manufac turer's championship win.

The following year the Audi tear were faced with the new Lancia 03 which in the right driving hands woul prove formidable, although the car me its match in the Quattro. The season' racing was a tightly run contest but th Quattro had the slight edge under th supervision of Mikkola who won th World Championship in 1983. The fac that Lancia was performing so we arguably made some critics wonde about the four-wheel drive Audi, how ever, the following season Rohrl decide to abandon the Lancia "ship" and th team lost their star driver. Their loss wa Audi's gain but a new threat was on th horizon in the form of the Peugeot 20 Turbo 16 which was a lightweight per

ABOVE Action from the RAC Rally, 1983

manent four-wheel drive with serious intents on taking the championship. While the teams were battling it out for supremacy in the Group B races, other plans were being discussed behind the scenes. This would involve changing the Group B rules and bringing the pace of Rally racing down a notch or two. It

ABOVE Sport S1
Quattro, 1987

wasn't going to be easy and Michele Mouton, for one, was a driver who didn't want to slow down the exciting speed of Rallying. However, several accidents had hampered the sport for a while and it was decided that a new type of racing should be introduced. The result was the Group A rules in 1986. Mouton, clearly disappointed and exasperated with the decision to end Group B racing

effectively quit the sport.

Racing continued and during 1984, Audi continued to shine, especially with the wins clocked up by Stig Blomqvist and the quiet man from Sweden was honoured that year by winning the World Championship while Audi claimed the coveted constructors' championship award. It was a resoundingly successful year for the team but yet more threats were looming. Yes, other teams were advancing and gaining ground on Audi who had proved over the previous four years that they were undoubtedly one of, if not the best in the sport, but this was not the ultimate problem. The biggest threat the team faced was the expense of running, managing and maintaining a full racing programme. At the same time, simply giving up and letting their competitors run them out of the race was not an option and Audi's answer, as with any other racing outfit, was a new car.

The Sport Quattro was an extreme car - it needed to be in what were essentially extreme times. The engine of the original Quattro was upgraded and the bodywork was lightweight although the suspension was kept much the same. Despite the efforts of Audi to make the car much lighter than the Quattro, the Sport was still reasonably heavy compared to other racing vehicles. Another drawback appeared to be the concentration required to drive the car and there seemed to be little praise for the new, hopefully winning, formula. Even the experienced Audi team drivers were unsure about the car's handling and improvements were a pre-requisite.

While the car was being worked on and upgraded, Audi was finding itself left behind on the track.

Following Michele Mouton's "retirement" from racing and the introduction of Group A rules for the 1987 season, cars were designed to resemble their road counterparts more closely and the ferocious speeds and fighting ability of the previous cars was somewhat calmed down. The main contenders, including Audi were still in the running and the four-wheel drive vehicles were faring better overall than the rear-wheel drive machines. For Audi, who were gaining just as much success and failure as many of the other principal teams, the latest car to try its wow factor on the track was a Quattro saloon with a five cylinder turbocharged engine. It would prove to be a decent enough vehicle to master some success and appropriate wins but, even after the Sport, nothing seemed to conjure up the same dramatic scenes and exciting tempo that the original Quattro had managed. The Quattro had made a splash when it entered Group B rules in 1981, stunning spectators and the racing fraternity alike. Audi had never before made an impact like it and it seemed very unlikely that they would do again.

Chapter 8

The Races: A History

1000 Lakes Rally
(Rally Finland)

TODAY, THE RALLY HELD IN FINland each year is known as the Neste Oil Rally Finland named after its sponsor Neste Oil. However, when Quattro was heading the field, the race was more commonly known as the 1000 Lakes Rally. Held in the Jyvaskyla area of the country, the race is more affectionately known by the locals as the Jyvaskylan Suurajot or Great Race.

The first Rally was held here in 1951 when it was a national event won by Arvo Karlsson with co-driver Vilho Mattila in an Austin Atlantic. But, since the introduction of the World Championships in 1973, the race became part of a historic European event and was referred to as the "Gravel Grand Prix" because of the high speed track which these days, attracts more than 500,000 spectators. The Rally is one of the most prestigious events on the calendar and is the largest organised meet in all three Nordic countries.

One of the most renowned stages in the race comes in the Ouninpohja which features high speed jumps and has a maximum average speed of 115 mph as dictated by the FIA. However, because this was exceeded in the 2004 Rally, the section was then split into two parts. This was reversed for the 2007 Rally, but the 2008 Rally meant that the two parts were again installed. The course of the race is extremely difficult. So difficult in fact that only three drivers who were not from Finland, Norway or Sweden have ever won the Rally; these comprise, Markko Martin with co-driver Michael

LEFT The main straight at night of the 24 hour Le Mans Rally

Park (from Germany and the UK respectively) in 2003 driving a Ford Focus RS WRC 03, Frenchmen Didier Auriol and co-driver Bernard Occelli in a Lancia Delta HF Integrale and Spaniards Carlos Sainz and Luis Moya in 1990 driving a Toyota Celica. The course has four times been voted as the World Rally Championship "Rally of the Year" in 1998, 2002, 2003 and 2004. The Rally was held in 2008 between 31 July and 3 August in the central Finnish location and was the ninth time that the course had hosted a World Rally Championship event.

Le Mans

THE 24-HOUR LE MANS RALLY IS one of the most renowned on the racing calendar and is a real test of endurance for both drivers and vehicles. The race officially began in the French town in the department of Sarthe in 1923 and has been held near the town of Le Mans ever since. Affectionately known as the "Grand Prix of Endurance", Le Mans is organised by the French club, Automobile Club de l'Ouest (ACO), with a circuit containing closed public

roads which lasts over 24 hours and tests drivers' abilities in speed and endurance. The Rally grew up alongside the formula Grand Prix but had a rather different edge. Instead of just testing the manufacturer's fastest machines and most able drivers, Le Mans was devised to test the sporting ability of cars, which had fuel efficiency while the length of the Mulsanne straight was incorporated to test drivers' speed. As some of the circuit is a public highway and not as "clean" and smooth as a racetrack would be, the cars are also put through their paces by the need for reliability on often bumpy surfaces.

By the late 1970s, further demands were put on drivers and manufacturers when the Group C rules were introduced at Le Mans, whereby cars were given a limited amount of fuel around which an engine needed to be designed. The fuel formulas were difficult to master and Group C was eventually abandoned. Fuel economy continued to be an important focus at Le Mans and, still is, into the 21st Century.

Around 50 competitors turn up at Le Mans each year to compete in the gruelling race with its stringent rules. Two seats must be present in each car and no

LEFT Scrutineering at Le Mans

RIGHT An aerial view
of the starting grid
during the Le Mans 24
Hours

more than two doors are allowed. Cars compete at the same time in different classes. The aim is to be the overall winner. Today there are four classes at Le Mans comprising custom-built Le Mans prototypes (two classes) and production grand tourers (two classes). Originally, the rules applying to drivers were more relaxed than they are today and there were no limitations on the number of drivers a car could have or how long they could drive. The 1980s and 1990s saw more and more safety guidelines and regulations brought into place and today, three drivers are deemed necessary to take part in the Rally. In the 1990s it was then decreed that drivers could not drive longer than four consecutive hours and no driver could drive for more than 14 hours in total. There are many unique rules and traditions associated with the Grand Prix of Endurance. As the Rally is a substantially long event, some regulations exist to ensure driver safety while others have been devised to help with, what is after all, a competition.

One of the many rules that grew up over the decades was that any car found to need refilling (in terms of oil and coolant, for example) in the first hour of Le Mans was disqualified as it was deemed unreliable. Another safety measure was also introduced when it was required that drivers switch off the engine while being refuelled. While mainly a safety rule, it was also to test any car's ability to be switched on and off a great many times under competition conditions. No other work may be carried out on the car while it is being refuelled. Le Mans has also been the venue for some (at the time) rather strange traditions which today are considered part of proceedings. In 1967, Dan Gurney and his co-driver won Le Mans and rather than drinking the champagne they were given on the podium, set about spraying it over the heads of all those standing nearby. Although it looked rather unusual at the time, this tradition is now synonymous with celebrating a great many sporting victories.

Le Mans is held in June each year (although in 1956 it took place in July and in 1968 in September). It was cancelled in 1936 due to the Great Depression and from 1940 to 1948 because of hostilities during the Second World War. Qualifying and practice takes place a few days before the race

LEFT Victory for the Audi team at Le Mans, June 2007

LEFT Monte Carlo Rally start, 1912

weekend and in previous years there was a qualifying session held in April or May. There have been some variations in the time the Rally has started over the years, but the standard time for Le Mans to start was at 4.00 pm on the Saturday. The 2008 Rally began at 3.00 pm and it is thought that this new time will stand for future rallies.

In earlier decades, race results were determined by how far a car had travelled but these days winners are judged by the number of laps they achieve. The car must cross the finish line after 24 hours of racing to qualify for the final results listings having completed a set distance within the last hour of the race (to avoid any damaged or "limping" vehicles to wait in the pits until the 24 hours are up, only to cross the finishing line looking for a result).

The actual circuit at Le Mans is called the Circuit de la Sarthe and is a mixture of both permanent track and public roads running at about nine miles in length. Some modifications have been made to the track over the years, some quite recently, including on the Mulsanne when the FIA declared that no straight on any circuit could be longer than one and a half miles in

length. The Mulsanne duly had two chi-
canes added on its three and a half mile
straight. The public roads offer drivers
and vehicles less grip due to the heavy
traffic that they support during the rest
of the year. These roads are also not as

well maintained as the remainder of the
circuit and require a large number of
safety barriers to be put up and down
literally within hours of the start and
finish of the race. It was somewhat different when Le Mans hosted its first

official race in 1923. Only public roads were used around the town of Le Mans itself with the winner having to compete three years in a row to claim the coveted title. This was abandoned in 1928 when it was decreed that a winner (who had travelled the greatest distance) would be awarded the title on an annual basis. The first years of Le Mans were dominated by the British, French and Italians and by the 1940s and 1950s was a highlight of the European calendar. However, the race is not without its tragedy and in 1955, 80 people were killed when a car ploughed into a crowd of spectators. It was Ford in the 1960s that took Le Mans to new heights with fast speeds in their production vehicles. But, these cars were set to be superseded by the all-new, purpose built sports cars that would come to dominate the 1970s. The following decade it was Porsche who dominated the circuit at Le Mans.

The 1990s brought its own changes when the so-called super sports cars were seemingly in demise. It was back to the production-based cars of earlier years who began to dominate once again including the likes of Audi, BMW, Ferrari, Mercedes-Benz, Toyota, Mazda and Nissan, to name but a few.

As costs of racing spiralled ever upwards only the elite could afford to keep a racing programme on track and Audi have begun to dominate in the 21st Century with the R8. In 2005, Audi introduced the diesel engine prototype – the R10 TDI – which was the first ever diesel powered vehicle to claim a victory at Le Mans.

Monte Carlo Rally

RALLYE AUTOMOBILE MONTE CARlo, or the Monte Carlo Rally, is an important event on the World Rally Championship calendar. Organised by the Automobile Club de Monaco, the race is held each year along the French Riviera in the Principality of Monaco. Located in south east France, Monte Carlo was first added to the European racing scene in 1911 by Prince Albert I. It is renowned for its difficult and demanding conditions which require endurance and stamina along with a high level of concentration amongst the drivers as well as an innovative approach (regulations allowing) from

LEFT Walter Rohrl (R) and his teammate Christian Geistdorfer pose next to their car prior to the Monte Carlo Rally, 1983

ABOVE West-German driver Walter Rohrl

the team. Like many other rallies, the race in Monte Carlo is not just about speed, but about the team's ability to produce a reliable car that can demonstrate the latest improvements that can be tested to the limit. Any win at Monte Carlo assures the driver and manufacturer of much sought after publicity. It is a particularly prestigious event and a win here is held in high regard.

The Rally became part of the World Rally Championship at the inaugural season in 1973 and has traditionally been the first race each year, held in January. The event allowed drivers for many years to pick a starting point equidistant from Monaco although all drivers had to finish in the same place. The terrain was different over the course of the race and could comprise tarmac (wet and dry), snow and ice and tyre choices were crucial to success or failure. The most renowned stage of the Monte Carlo Rally is from La Bollene to Sospel which takes the competitor over a steep, winding mountain with virtual hairpin bends. It is extremely gruelling for the drivers, especially over the Col de Turini which is usually covered in ice and snow. The "Night of Turini" is extremely popular with spectators who come in their droves to watch the drivers tackle the exciting and often dangerous stretch of the race. Due to the high beams from the cars' headlights, this part of the event is also referred to as the night of the long knives. Drivers and spectators alike were disappointed when the stage through the Turini was abandoned for the 2007 event, however, the stage was included once again in January 2008.

BELOW West-German driver Walter Rohrl (2dL) and his teammate Christian Geistdorfer (L) jubilant on the podium after winning the Monte Carlo Rally, 1984

LEFT The car named
after the hillclimb

Pikes Peak International Hill climb

THE RACE TO THE CLOUDS, AS IT is commonly known, is officially named the Pikes Peak International Hillclimb and is the annual Rally, held unsurprisingly, at Pikes Peak, Colorado in the US. Comprising more than 12 gruelling miles with more than 156 turns while climbing more than 4,700 feet, the race was first introduced to the racing calendar in 1916 and is open to cars, trucks, motorcycles and quads. There are usually around 150 competitors in the race that was originally initiated, organised and promoted by Spencer Penrose. He was responsible for widening the Pikes Peak road into a highway and to encourage visitors and tourists (as well as locals) to see the benefits of the pass, he decided to hold a race named the "Race to the Clouds". In 1916, the winner was Rea Lentz who managed the climb in 20:55.40. However, the current overall record is held by Nobuhiro Tajima from Japan who won the race in

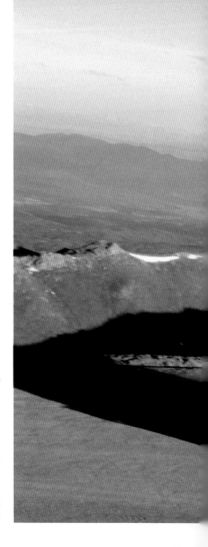

RIGHT Audi action at
Pikes Peak

just 10:01.408 in July 2007.

Except for one or two races, the Race to the Clouds is held on 4 July each year, and ties in well with national celebrations. There are various classes for cars and trucks including the unlimited "anything goes" category, open wheel, super stock car and pro trucks while motorcycles and quads can enter the 1200cc, 750cc, quad 500, quad 450 and motorcycle sidecar categories to name but a few.

Tour de Corse

HELD ON THE ISLAND OF CORSICA for the first time in 1956, the Tour de Corse became a World Rally Championship course that was originally developed over the island's road network. Today, the race is conducted around the roads of Ajaccio. Also known as the "Ten Thousand Turns Rally", because of the numerous mountain roads that the course covers, the Rally is held on asphalt and several unlucky drivers have died as a result of taking part here. The outstanding driver Henri Toivonen was one, as was Attilio Bettega; both died here during the mid-1980s. The first winners of the

Tour de Corse when the Rally became part of the World Championship were Jean-Pierre Nicolas and Michel Vial from France in 1973 driving an Alpine Renault A110 1800. The most recent winner was the Frenchman Sebastien Loeb with co-driver Daniel Elena from Monaco in a Citroen C4. It was not the first win on the island for Loeb, who had won the race on two other occasions with his dedicated co-driver in 2005 and 2006; on the two earlier occasions Loeb had been driving a Citroen Xsara.

Wales GB Rally
(The RAC Rally)

THE RAC RALLY AS IT WAS KNOWN until 1999 is the largest and most prolific of the races conducted in the UK. When the name changed, the race became known as the Wales Rally GB, partly because of its location in and around the city of Cardiff in Wales and partly due to sponsorship. The race first came to fruition in 1933 when 367 teams entered the Royal Automobile Club Rally which began from nine different towns and cities across the country including London, Liverpool,

Newcastle, Edinburgh, Bath, Leamington Spa, Buxton and Harrogate. The race, from each city, was devised to be around 1,000 miles long and each competitor was expected to finish in the seaside resort of Torquay in Devon. The race, however, was not just one of speed and drivers were expected to show their skills in acceleration and

LEFT The challenging Pikes Peak course

ABOVE Sebastian Loeb has won the race on the island of Corsica in recent years

although the finish in Torquay was changed to Hastings in East Sussex. Winners were generally picked on the least penalties they had managed to acquire over the length of the course.

Up until 1939, the Rally was an annual event but the Second World War halted the yearly status of the race as it did with almost every other sporting event in the country. In 1951, the race was once again on the annual racing calendar although the Suez Crisis and an outbreak of foot and mouth stopped the race in 1957 and 1967 respectively. Interestingly, UK winners have dominated the event while the Nordic countries have fared quite well over the years. The only other nationalities to celebrate winners on rare occasions have been the Japanese, French and Germans to name the majority. The Forestry Commission allowed a two mile section of forest roads in Scotland to be used in the race and it was to be a turning point for the competition. The success of the two mile stretch meant that other forest roads were opened up across the country for the following year's event in 1961.

By the start of the following decade, spectators were being invited to join in

braking as well as slow running. There was no overall winner for the first RAC Rally. The overall format of the race was then adopted for subsequent years

the fun and stages were set up along various routes in parks and private estates where the general public could come and cheer on the competitors. Unlike the forest roads, these events were unpopular with the drivers because parading past spectators waving and cheering did little to provide a competitive edge to the race. As the race matured, the RAC Rally became an important part of the World Rally Championships. Sponsorship was to prove a fairly new concept in the early 1970s with the *Daily Mirror* becoming the first official sponsor of the event. Other sponsors over the years have contributed to the financial success of the Rally and have come from a number of businesses and financial institutions. One of the main sponsors was Lombard North Central and the event soon became renamed as the Lombard RAC Rally. Today, with sponsorship from the Welsh Development Agency the Rally is officially called the Wales Rally GB.

Tragedy struck at the 2005 rally when Michael "Beef" Park, the co-driver for Markko Martin died having sustained injuries on the final leg of the race. He had only just joined the Peugeot team and was considered one of the top co-

FAR LEFT Lombard were the sponsors of the Wales Rally for a number of years

LEFT A car drives through the Welsh hills, 1999

drivers of his peers. The event in 2007 was the 75th Wales Rally GB (formerly RAC Rally) and was held between November and December that year. The final round of the World Rally Championship takes place in December 2008.

World Rally Championship

THE WORLD RALLY CHAMPION-ship (WRC) is organised by the FIA and offers both drivers and manufacturers the chance of winning the coveted titles at the end of the racing season. Although the drivers' and manufacturers' championships are separate, both are run on the same points system which came into effect in 1973 with the first ever World Rally Championship. The inaugural season in the early 1970s began with the Monte Carlo Rally held in January. That year, 13 rallies in total were held although today, only seven of the original events remain including, Monte Carlo, Rally Finland (1000 Lakes Rally), Wales Rally GB (RAC Rally), Tour de Corse, the Swedish Rally,

Acropolis Rally and Rally Portugal.

The first drivers' championship was not won until 1979 when victory was claimed by the Swede, Bjorn Waldegard, although the FIA Cup for Drivers was presented to Sandro Munari and Markku Alen in 1977 and 1978 respectively. In 1973, however, the manufacturer's championship was awarded to Alpine Renault for the Alpine A110 while the following three years saw Lancia claim the title. In 2007, the World Championships comprised 16 rallies which took place over gravel, tarmac and on two occasions, snow. Norway took part for the first time in the same year, along with fellow newcomer Ireland. Portugal was also back in the frame after a period of absence from the competition. Rally Australia, Cyprus and Turkey did not take part (although Australia will be back in the championship during 2009). In 2008, there were 15 rallies in the championship and Jordan was the newcomer while Turkey made a comeback. The three "newcomers" for 2007 – Norway, Ireland and the prodigal Portugal – were not part of the 2008 season.

The championships have their own rules and regulations and each car is

LEFT Acropolis Rally during the World Rally Championships

built to specific guidelines. All cars are required to be production based 2.0 litre turbocharged four-wheel drives and the power output today has been limited to 300 bhp (225 kW). The current cars in the WRC races include Peugeot, Citroen, Ford, Skoda, Suzuki and Subaru. It was 1986 that marked a turning point in WRC racing when a series of fatal accidents led to regulations being revised. Although safety measures had been increased over the preceding years, the speed of the cars on the circuits had also been increasing. Group B races, particularly, were becoming death-defying events.

Group B racing took off during the 1980s with the introduction of four-wheel drive vehicles from Audi (initially) and then other competitors who were keen to develop the idea once the Audi team had consistently demonstrated that the concept worked in practice. Group B rules were introduced in 1982 but the few restrictions there were meant that manufacturers were free to lead the way with almost unlimited power. Group B cars were banned from competition in 1987. The planned Group S regulations fared no better and

so the Group A rules became the standard regulations for Rally driving. (These remained in place until 1997.) It was Lancia who adapted the most quickly to the new rules and so went on to dominate the championships; the team won the constructors' championship six times in succession. By the 1990s, new teams were

LEFT Action in the mountains of the Acropolis Rally during the World Rally Championships

beginning to have the technology to rival the Lancia. Toyota, Mitsubishi and Subaru were all in the running for the championship titles and Toyota, in particular, had success with Carlos Sainz from Spain who won the drivers' championship in 1990 and 1992. Victory was Toyota's again in 1994 but Subaru and Mitsubishi were not far behind.

The end of the decade then brought new changes and the World Rally Car regulations came into effect (replacing Group A rules) in 1998. This time, it was the turn of Peugeot to win through and the team won both championships at the end of the 1990s.

Chapter 9

The Rally Drivers

Stig Blomqvist

RIGHT Stig Blomqvist in action, 1983

THE SAAB RALLY TEAM, ALTHOUGH under-funded compared with its rivals, were the lucky ones to gain the talent of Stig Blomqvist. The team did not remain in the professional championships, however, the illustrious career of Blomqvist was set to continue. His brief stint with Talbot led him to Audi following a test session which quite literally wowed the team bosses. What really made Blomqvist stand out was his ability to use left-foot breaking in order to negotiate a four-wheel vehicle into actually sliding around corners. His style was incredibly fast and his performance simply staggered the crowds. By the 1983 racing season he was the quickest Audi team member. The downfall, unfortunately, was that a lack of mechanical reliability saw the championship title ebb away from the outstanding racing driver.

But, 1984 was to prove rather different. In fact, it was to be the year for the talented Blomqvist who worked hard at beating his rivals. His natural talent shone through and the drivers' title was his in that same year. It would prove to be a winning formula for Audi who also picked up the constructor's championship too.

John Buffum

IF AMERICAN JOHN BUFFUM HAD declined the offer of navigating in a borrowed MGA with a college team mate on a time, speed, distance Rally in 1964, the world would never have known one of the greatest (if not the

RIGHT John Buffum drove an Audi 80 before success with the Quattro

ABOVE Hannu Mikkola drove this car in 1985

most famous US driver) of all time. The experience was a turning point for Buffum who, two years later with his then wife and co-driver Vicki Gauntlett, became a regular on the TSD circuit. It was the start of an exciting career that would see him win the New England Winter Rally just a year later in a Mini-

Cooper as co-driver for Tim Gold.

Buffum graduated from college and joined the US Army as a mechanical engineer. He was sent to Germany with the Engineer Corps having been promoted to second lieutenant. It was to further his interest in Rallying when he witnessed world racing for the first time. The talented American went out and bought a Porsche 911T so that he too could compete in both international and regional rallies and in 1969 he secured a 12th place win at the Monte Carlo Rally when he co-drove with fellow American Steve "Yogi" Behr. Professional Rallying did not, at this time, exist in the US and on his return home in 1970 he turned to IMSA and SCCA road racing in order to repeat the thrill and speeds which European racing had given him a taste for. He then formed his own racing outfit, Libra Racing and used a Mini and Ford Escort for team Rallying. Steve Behr was a regular in the car with Buffum, as were the likes of George Follmer and Brett Lunger. However, the team didn't have the right car to propel them onto the winners' podium although there were some top 10 finishes.

Performance Rallying was just beginning to follow Europe by the mid-1970s in the US and although divorced from his wife in 1974, Buffum and Vicki continued to work together on the track. In 1975, the Libra team used a Porsche and then came some hard-earned recognition. Buffum and his ex-wife won three important rallies, two in the US and one in Canada and this took them to the NARRA national championship. Meanwhile, Buffum's style was beginning to show his true potential and he was fast gaining a reputation as a championship driver. He continued to impress and became known for his capabilities over the ever-changing Rally conditions. In 1977 Buffum chose a Triumph TR-7 and TR-8 for the team and secured commitment from Doug Shepherd as his co-driver. It was to prove a winning formula.

The two men stormed through the SCCA Pro Rally series and the North American Rally Championship. Next Buffum and Shepherd worked with an Audi 80 and a Peugeot 504, but neither car was able to match the current "new kid on the block" the Mazda RX-7. For 12 months there was great disappointment until Audi supplied the team with the new Audi Quattro in 1982. The combination was to prove electric and there was no looking back for the team. There was still competition from the Mazda, but the Quattro, then the Quattro A2 and finally the Sport Quattro were proving more than a match for the previous fast car – no matter how many improvements and

RIGHT Hannu Mikkola in an Audi Quattro at the RAC Rally

greater engine capacity the Mazda received. Buffum still liked to race in Europe and in 1983 he became the only American to have ever won a European event when he claimed the European Championship title. Buffum next took on Tom Grimshaw with whom he enjoyed even greater success winning championship after championship during 1987 which left Buffum with the honour of being the most acclaimed winner of rallies across the globe. He had 104 national victories at this time and he retired on a high from driving. His commitment remained in the sport and Buffum became a SCCA Pro Rally series manager. Today, Buffum still manages Libra Racing and supports his stepson, Paul Choiniere, who drove several Audis before driving a Hyundai Tiburon. Buffum has also contributed to the sport as a coachbuilder and engineer as well as having been the American Rally Association's president. He has also been instrumental in event organisation, including the Maine Forest Rally in the US and the Mount Washington Hillclimb Auto Race. Born on 4 October 1943, Buffum eventually claimed 11 national titles and 117 national championship wins.

Hannu Mikkola

WITH A RALLY CAREER SPANNING more than 30 years and a World Championship under his belt, the Finn Hannu Mikkola is undoubtedly one of the world's most renowned drivers. Born in Joensuu on 24 May 1942, Mikkola was also a seven times winner of the 1000 Lakes Rally in his native country as well as a multiple winner of the RAC Rally. He began his career in a Volvo PV 544 in 1963, but the decade seemed to deprive the Finnish driver of any illustrious titles. However, in 1970 things started to look up in his customary Ford Escort. In 1977, he was joined by co-driver Arne Hertz and it was then that Mikkola began to come into his own. By 1979, he was almost World Champion; he eventually finished the competition just one point behind Bjorn Waldegard. He was signed to Ford for the 1980 season, but the following year, keeping his promise to Audi, Mikkola took up the season in a four-wheel drive Audi Quattro. It was to prove the making of the Finn. He led the 1981 Monte Carlo Rally (it was the Quattro's first outing) although a later

LEFT Hannu Mikkola in action at Pikes Peak

ABOVE Hannu Mikkola

RIGHT Michele
Mouton in 2008

the World Championship. But, 1983 would be the Finn's year. After four wins and three second places teammates, Mikkola and Hertz claimed the World Championship title. Mikkola would remain with Audi until 1987 before moving to Mazda.

Although Mikkola semi-retired in 1991, he remained with Mazda and continued to make some appearances at international rallies. He eventually retired from racing in 1993.

Michele Mouton

THE FRENCH-BORN RALLY DRIVER Michele Mouton is undoubtedly the most renowned female racing driver of all time. Born on 23 June 1951 in Grasse, Mouton began her career in 1974 driving her own private Alpine Renault and went on to become the only woman to win a World Championship Rally, which she achieved at the San Remo Rally in 1981. The following year saw Mouton have a stunning season in which several wins in Brazil, Acropolis and

accident put paid to hopes of both Mikkola and Audi. He went on to win the Swedish Rally and the RAC Rally. In 1982, despite wins in the 1000 Lakes Rally and, again, the RAC Rally, Mikkola still finished third overall in

Portugal, saw her, and her Quattro S1 narrowly miss claiming the World Rally Championship which went to Walter Rohrl driving an Opel.

The preceding years had also caused excitement for Mouton and her supporters. Success had come to the young Frenchwoman almost immediately in both French and European rallies as soon as she began in competition. Then in 1977, driving a Porsche Carrera RS she claimed her first international win at the Rally in Spain. There was more success in a Fiat 131 Abarth as well as a Lancia Stratos HF and Mouton established herself amongst the racing elite as a fearless driver in a male-dominated world. Then in 1981, Mouton joined Audi and was one of the first drivers, alongside team-mate Mikkola, to drive the revolutionary Audi Quattro. The car suffered some teething problems and mechanical unreliability before Mouton joined forces with co-driver Fabrizia Pons. Many would argue that it was Mouton who bravely took the four-wheel drive concept into racing – with a little help from Audi – which was to set the scene for racing in the decades to follow. Records and accolades followed and, in 1985, Mouton was the first

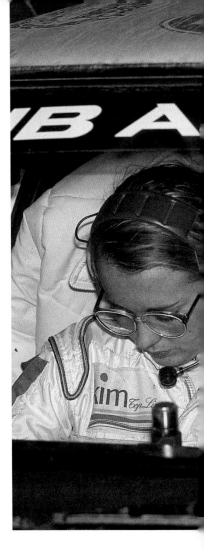

RIGHT Michele Mouton and Fabrizia Pons in action in their Audi during the RAC Rally of Great Britain, 1984

woman to win the Pikes Peak International Hillclimb race in the US. She basically decided to give up her career in 1986 when Group B racing was abandoned and Group A formula (with its different rules) took its place. Mouton was instrumental in organising the Race of Champions 1988 in memory of racing driver Henri Toivonen who was killed while taking part in the Tour de Corse when his car left the road and crashed. Toivonen had been leading the Rally and his death was a tremendous loss to the racing fraternity. As an Audi team Rallying legend, Mouton was an equal alongside her team-mates Hannu Mikkola and Walter Rohrl.

Walter Rohrl

BORN ON 7 MARCH 1947 IN REgensburg, Germany, Walter Rohrl had an exciting career for Audi, Fiat, Opel, Lancia, Porsche, Ford and BMW. His first job was as a driver – he was just 16 – however, it was not on the racetrack. Rohrl took a job as the Bishop of Regensburg's driver and was covering around 90,000 miles a year.

Rohrl was a sporty man (he was par-

RIGHT Walter Rohrl prior to the Monte Carlo Rally, 1983

FAR RIGHT Rohrl in action during Portuguese Rally, 1985

ticularly active in skiing) and was invited to drive in his first Rally in 1968. It was to lead to a rather different career and during the following two decades, Rohrl won the Monte Carlo Rally four times (in four different cars). He had numerous successes in the Opel Ascona 400 rear-wheel drive, but was lured to Lancia where he was to test drive the Lancia 037. This vehicle, also rear-wheel drive would dominate for a while (alongside the Ford Escort) but he was tempted by the Quattro and in 1984 he joined Audi. Rohrl also liked road racing events.Overall, Rohrl competed in 75 World Rally Champion-ship races and won the title twice, in 1980 and 1982

He claimed 31 podium finishes and 420 stage wins scoring 494 points throughout his 14 year career. He was renowned for being selective in the races that he competed in and this is a good score for the man who last won at the 1985 San Remo Rally in 1985. Rohrl's last world Rally was the Acropolis Rally in 1987; the same year that he retired.

Chapter 10

The Quattro In A Modern World

SUCH IS THE APPEAL OF THE ORIginal quattro, that the 25th anniversary of the car's launch was celebrated in 1986. There are also owners clubs for the Quattro (www.quattroownersclub.com) – who organise events and provide helpful advice and information – and Audis in general (www.clubaudi.co.uk) so whatever you drive you're always guaranteed a friendly reception.

While it is still possible to pick up a quality Quattro coupe for less than £10,000 (a Sport Quattro will probably set you back more than £50,000 even if you are lucky enough to find one for sale), the chances are that you might be more interested in Audi's more recent cars in which the Quattro heritage lives on.

Indeed, the Quattro four-wheel drive system is prevalent in Audi's fleet of cars. It either comes as standard or is an optional extra on almost every model on offer as the first decade of the 21st Century comes to an end, from a small hatchback like the A3 through to family saloons (and their derivatives such as estates) like the A4, A5 or the A6 to the luxury executive saloon that is the A8. Of course, you might want to go the whole hog and drive around in a more traditional 4x4 such as the Q5 or Q7 but if you want to truly experience the thrill of driving a four-wheel drive sports car then why not choose the TT or the R8.

The TT (Tourist Trophy) was

The new Audi TT 3.2 litre V-6 engine with 4 valves per cylinder,
variable camshaft timing and variable intake manifold

3.189 cm^3
184 kW (250 PS) @ 6.300 min^{-1}
320 Nm @ 2.500 - 3.000 min^{-1}

ABOVE The Audi TT 3.2
V6 engine with 4 valves
per cylinder, variable
camshaft timing and
variable intake
manifold

launched at the 1995 Tokyo Motor
Show but it took another three years
before it came into production. The TT
was offered in two formats; a two-plus-
two coupe (September 1998) and a two
seater roadster (August 1999) but both
boasted blistering pace although reports
of high speed crashes led to the cars
being recalled to improve their road
handling. An initial choice of 20-valve
four-cylinder 1,781cc engines gave
potential buyers the option to go for
either 180 bhp or 225 bhp depending on
their preference (and budget) while the

interior was immaculately designed and crafted. Once again, Audi had led the way with the competitors struggling to catch up.

Launched in 2005, the second generation TTs were offered with a choice of

2.0 litre or 3.2 litre engines with a six-speed manual or tronic gearbox. In 2008, it was announced that the TT could also be fitted with a 2.0 diesel engine, which would give the coupe an average fuel consumption of around 45 miles to the gallon.

Audi's 1998 acquisition of Lamborghini, however, brought an exciting development to the Audi range in the form of the R8. Audi's technological resources had helped to produce one of the most desirable cars ever made in the Lamborghini Murcielago in 2001 but,

with only 3,066 built to the end of 2007 and a £160,000 price tag, the German company saw a gap in the market that needed filling so developed their own mid-engined sports car.

The two-seater coupe R8 was unveiled to the world at the Paris Motor Show in 2006 and production began the

BELOW Audi A6 all road Quattro

following year (rumours persist that a roadster will be announced in 2009). It wasn't long before the production total of the Murcielago was surpassed...not surprising seeing as the R8 retails at around £80,000 and is equipped with a 4.2 litre FSI V8 engine that develops 420 PS. It has also been hailed as the first serious rival to Porsche's world domination of the sports car market since they launched their 911 in 1964. In an echo that harks back to the Quattro Coupe, 70 skilled workers assemble 5,000 of the car's parts by hand and the factory produces just 25 cars a day.

In a move that would have baffled designers of sports cars in years gone by, early 2008 saw a diesel engined version being presented at the North American International and Geneva Motor Shows. Labelled the R8 TDI Le Mans, its six litre V12 engine produces 500 PS which, meshed to a six-speed manual gearbox, enables the car to accelerate from 0-62 mph in 4.2 seconds, with its top speed being 202 mph.

Whatever the future holds for Audi, in the immortal words of a recent mobile phone advertising campaign, you can be sure that it will be bright.

LEFT The R8 Tdi Le Mans, 2008

LEFT The Audi R8

Other books also available:

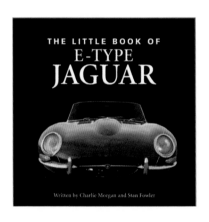

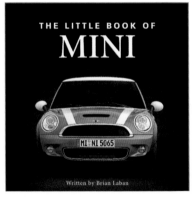

The pictures in this book were provided courtesy of the following:

GETTY IMAGES
101 Bayham Street, London NW1 0AG

SHUTTERSTOCK IMAGES
www.shutterstock.com

Design and artwork by David Wildish

Creative Director: Kevin Gardner

Image Research: Ellie Charleston

Published by Green Umbrella Publishing

Publishers Jules Gammond and Vanessa Gardner

Written by Charlie Morgan and Stan Fowler